DON'T BE WEIRD

DON'T BE WEIRD

Stories and Strategies on How to Lead

People to Jesus Anytime & Anywhere

Ellaine S. Ursuy

TABLE OF CONTENTS

Editor's Note: 9

Dedication   11

Preface: Dating   13
Analogies to get used to

SECTION 1   19
WHERE I AM COMING FROM

CHAPTER ONE   21
Testimony

CHAPTER TWO   33
Who Jesus is to me

SECTION 2   39
WHY

CHAPTER THREE   41
Elevated Surfaces

CHAPTER FOUR   45
Being Comfy

CHAPTER FIVE   49
Don't Freak Out

CHAPTER SIX   53
Knowing Jesus is to do this

CHAPTER SEVEN   59
A Relevant Pause

CHAPTER EIGHT   63
Fruits

SECTION 3 75
OVERCOMING OBSTACLES

CHAPTER NINE 77
Tantrums

CHAPTER TEN 83
Who needs this?

SECTION 4 91
WHAT

CHAPTER ELEVEN 93
Table to Stand on or Book Nook to cuddle into

CHAPTER TWELVE 101
My Version of the story

CHAPTER THIRTEEN 107
The Ask

CHAPTER FOURTEEN 113
Curveball

CHAPTER FIFTEEN 119
Let Him stick His flag in us, not ours in others.

CHAPTER SIXTEEN 125
Your Plan

SECTION 5 129
GO NOW!

CHAPTER SEVENTEEN 131
Now

A Note From The Author 135

Editor's Note:

"I had the honor of playing a small role in this journey, and what a beautiful journey it has been! Ellaine's book definitely shines light on the everyday life of how we're called to live as Christians, and I believe more people need to hear it. It's authentic, powerful, and truthful. It definitely makes you think twice about why you're put here on this earth. Living for Jesus is not always perfect, but it's always worth it. We are flawed human beings, and it's incredible that Jesus chooses us over and over again to be used by Him. Even through our brokenness, He lifts us up higher and uses us in mighty ways to reach His people. I hope this book will change your life!"- Ana Bohr

Ana Bohr- a 26 year old, digital creator, based in Orange County, California. Originally from Grand Rapids, Michigan, she moved to California in 2018 to be a part of a local church plant, 'Hillsong Church'. She now contracts for the church globally, providing social media services, and runs her own business on the side. She assists clients with all backgrounds growing their business through digital services such as: virtual assistance, creative direction, authentic social media interaction, Pinterest, and blog management.

Follow her on IG: @anamariebohr or shoot her an Email: ana@upholdmagazine.com for more info!

Dedication

For my friend and colleague, Lauren Ballema Markel.

A woman who showed me that even through life's biggest trials, the best way we can spend our time is to share Jesus with anyone who will listen. Sometimes, insisting with those who don't want to listen at all.

Shortly after Lauren was diagnosed with DIPG, a rare brain tumor that is most often fatal, we were on campus together.

Why was this woman who was so sick on campus? She wouldn't have had it any other way. Her heart was to see everyone within her reach come to know Jesus, nothing would stop her.

We were at a cafeteria on the campus of WMU and as she was getting her lunch she engaged the person who was serving her in a conversation about Jesus.

When she came to sit down with me, I asked how it went.

"I led with telling him I have a brain tumor, so he kind of had to listen."

Lauren laughed so hard, as she often did, I didn't have time to be shocked. Honestly, that was the first of many times Lauren would tell me a story like that over the course of the next few years working together.

She went to be with Jesus just as I was about to publish. Paralyzed with fear and sadness, I didn't want to hit 'publish'. I know though from having known Lauren, there is no excuse to hold back the gospel.

I pray that as you read this book, we would grow the tenacity and contagious sort of faith that Lauren showed me.

"I will not die but live and proclaim all that the Lord has done." Psalm 118: 17

Preface: Dating

Analogies to get used to

My hope is that you picked up this book because you dream of learning about how to share the gospel with the people around you. My hope is that you will feel equipped to do that by the time you put this book down.

As I've written this book, my goal has been to communicate this in a way that is as relatable as possible. Not only to make it more readable but to help you understand that sharing the gospel does not have to be an uncomfortable experience.

You can expect to read more about who I am, so that you know where I am coming from. You can also expect to read more about why you should share the gospel at all. Finally, we will have a direct address of fears and questions which you may have, and how to actually go and do it.

I'm confident that God calls us all to go and share who He is with others, and I'm confident that I have had an absolute blast doing it. I'm also confident that you can too.

Dating

I've done a lot of it. A lot of it. Certainly enough to know the pattern off the top of my head (I guess "by heart" would be the more appropriate phrase here but *eye roll emoji*).

Example: Person A notices Person B. Person A approaches physically or via messaging app Person B, and they beat around the bush enough to be polite. Here is where the diversions start. (Spoiler alert- A is a good outcome. B, not so much).

A: They have fun chatting and continue bantering,

B: It goes to junk and someone is uncomfortable (hopefully it's mutual or at least one of them isn't in denial about it).

A: The banter becomes obviously more flirtatious

B: Someone has to awkwardly end the conversation and wham-bam, it's over before it started.

Someone pulls the trigger and asks the other person on a date

A: A "yes" is spoken

B: After that, the whole thing becomes a lot less predictable because well... people.

Why am I talking to you about dating in a book about how to talk to people about Jesus? I know from experience that it's a comparable scenario.

I guarantee that as you engage with the practice of putting yourself out there to make Him famous, you will feel uncomfortable.

Your palms will sweat. You will be nervous that you said the wrong thing. You will have to apologize once you've offended someone. Sometimes though, just sometimes, you will get to see someone start to fall in love with Jesus Himself.

Sales

The reality of both traditional sales and fundraising is usually when the product is good, it's easy to sell. Think about a time you bought something for someone that was an absolute no brainer (the last purchase or donation that was an immediate "Heck yes!").

Being salesy can come off like recommending things like the most recent hotel-grade memory foam we got to enjoy for our beds at home, or convincing others that they too need to own the name brand piece of clothing we just invested in.

In all honesty, we need to come to that place with Jesus. We need to be just as willing, if not more willing, to recommend Him to our friends and family.

Sales is something I've done a fair amount of. I worked in college ministry for 5 years and fundraising was the model that made the whole boat float.

Our fundraising responsibilities were to persuade friends and family to support the mission to the tune of $30,000-$70,000. By the time I finished working for InterVarsity, over 200 people had financially supported the work.

The process of sharing with someone who Jesus is to me can feel a little sales-y.

Particularly the actual "asking" part. When you are asking someone to commit to something, be it their money or their heart, asking once might not cut it.

They are both too hard to part with, you have to get good at what's referred to as "tarrying". All it means is this, you ask, give someone time to think, let them respond, and ask again but re-word it.

This is the part that feels kind of odd. You will likely think to yourself, "you're being annoying, they already said no". I promise you though, when people understand who Jesus is, they won't want to say no.

In fact, giving a person some time to think through such a weighty decision is the most appropriate thing you can do. Asking again is not manipulative or coercive, it's kind.

I often don't ask again as my next sentence, nor should you. A more appropriate question is, "Is there something specific that prevents you from wanting a relationship with Jesus?"

That's when the guts of the whole thing tend to come out. It's a wonderful way of revealing their fears and letting you know exactly what the true barrier is.

We will dig into that later but for now, know that this can bring up a bunch of feelings. Also, prepare because I will continue to use dating and sales analogies throughout this book.

SECTION 1

WHERE I AM COMING FROM

CHAPTER ONE

Testimony

To understand where exactly I am coming from, and why I'm so passionate about the subject, it might be helpful to know how I came to Jesus.

I need you to know that you are not allowed to read this part if you say "my testimony isn't that great" or "my testimony is more boring than that" at the end. Kapish?

Everyone's story of coming to know Jesus is a miracle. Period. To come to know the God of heaven and earth, the King of Kings, the Lord of Lords, is phenomenal in every way it happens.

To come to know that He just loves *you* is a miracle. No exceptions. Got that? No comparison allowed in the paragraphs below.

I'm going to start telling you about my life starting in middle school. It's not because I'm ashamed or because I'm hiding my life prior. It is because that's when I became more conscious of God and began to consider what His influence might be on my life.

I hung out with the academically advanced track crowd throughout middle and high school. This crowd had some epic people in it. We were an odd combo of pre-teens that cared deeply about each other.

Two friends in that group went to church, one Catholic, one Lutheran. I was curious about the Lutheran confirmation homework and asked if I could come along sometime. I attended and there were some cute boys so I kept attending.

I started to learn the books of the Bible and went to church twice a week. Often, I went mainly for extra activities throughout the week. I had to take notes on sermons each Sunday.

Sadly, throughout that year or so, I did not come to understand who Jesus was, much less know Him. No-fault to the church at all, I was a boy crazy 12-13-year-old girl dealing with acne with a ton of angst.

Come high school, I decided to attend a retreat with the other friend I mentioned through her catholic church. Again, I went because of cute boys.

We were in this gorgeous Victorian home with tons of tiny rooms. It had a staircase with spindles that elegantly led into a long and narrow living room not designed for the 30 of us there.

A young woman there shared her story. As she told us about her life, I found myself laughing and crying. All while she was telling her story, there was a 6 pack soda can holder, the plastic ones that don't end well for turtles, cut into a long strand, taped to a wood rafter (bold move), and burned.

Her story continued in a slow and dramatic tone, the flame burned purple, blue, green, and occasionally in ways, you couldn't see it. I listened intently sitting on the wood floor of this packed but beautiful living room. As she told the tough parts of her story, it happened to be that the flame wasn't visible.

I thought this was a complete fluke. She could not possibly have known the flame would burn in a way that we couldn't see it as she hit the tough spots.

Watching this happen though, and being 15-16, I took this to mean that God left in the hard times. Since I could not see that flame as she described the toughest parts of her life, I assumed God wasn't there.

I decided then that if that's who God was, I wanted nothing to do with Him.

Her take away was that even though sometimes we couldn't see the flame, it was still burning. Therefore, God was always present. I had already made my conclusions though and deemed it as ludacris as soon as it came out of her mouth.

Entering college (Fire Up, Chips!) I was on a leadership scholarship I was honored to have and involved in a handful of other organizations as well. Due to my scholarship and the reputation that came with it, I was quickly put into leadership positions in most of those organizations.

I just could not get enough affirmation no matter how many directions it was coming from. To add to the mix, I was also drinking 4-5 nights a week. I was in 3-4 leadership positions.

I was also making-out like it was a part-time job. I was getting free drinks in every bar and had more friends than I could reasonably hang out with and it was still never enough.

So naturally, to get more affirmation, I joined a sorority. My time in Alpha Gamma Delta was amazing. However, the beginning of my journey was terribly misguided. I planned to seek more boys, more booze, and more parties. I *needed* people to see me, and I *needed* to be affirmed.

Realistically, I think we all have this need. We may be confident, or even have an aura of "I don't care what people think about me" but in fact, we do care. Both of those things had always been true for me.

Yet, something in our hearts needed to know that we were validated and that other people see and know us as we are. There's this innate drive to know that we are good enough and that other people see that we are good enough.

I found the affirmation we are all seeking for in and through partying and leadership activities. I became philanthropy chair of my sorority shortly after my initiation.

I was also in "leadership" roles in multiple other organizations. I had the attention of more boys than ever before. I had more free booze than anyone could dream of. There was a problem though, it still wasn't enough.

There were a few women in the sorority though that seemed different. They seemed like they were content like they had some sort of secret in life that helped them to just rest assured.

These were the type of women who walk into a room and bring a sense of peace. Like in a movie, the star walks into the ballroom in the most perfect dress. Then, with that look of contentment on her face for the first time in the whole film, the whole room looks and is in awe of her.

That's what these women were like every day.

So, I asked them what was different about them.

They responded, without hesitation, that it was Jesus.

I asked if that was their boyfriend's name.

I was half-joking, but I was also pretty serious. If they were that content, that sure of themselves, that magnetic, this had to be an epic boyfriend that helped them know their worth.

They said it wasn't though, that Jesus, God, was what their contentment came from. I didn't believe it, so I kept living fast for a while.

A few months later, those same women invited me to a Greek Conference with them. It was a conference hosted by Greek InterVarsity Christian Fellowship.

An organization looking to see hearts renewed, lives transformed, and world-changers developed. They do this all through introducing fraternity and sorority students to Jesus in Bible studies led by their friends.

I wanted little to nothing to do with Jesus. But, these girls would not let up and about 12 hours before we got in the car to drive 6 hours to Indianapolis, I signed up to go.

Looking back at why I signed up is still crazy to me. I ended up feeling like I was supposed to go, which I now believe was the prompting of the Holy Spirit. Other things in my life weren't giving me the affirmation and fulfillment I so badly wanted.

I think some part of me knew that my friends throughout grade school had found that in religion and relationship with God. To be honest, I think I was getting tired of trying so hard all the time, I needed an out, an answer, and I was willing to look almost anywhere.

At the time though, my pride was too large to tell people that I was looking for anything at all. I felt like if I wasn't fulfilled, I was just a waste of space.

So, instead of admitting that I was looking for something more, I just told people (including my mom), that I might as well go. I mean it was $50 to stay in an astonishingly nice hotel. If all else failed, I would hang out in the hot tub and just go to the dance party.

This conference was nuts. There were 700 fraternity and sorority students at a 4-star hotel. There was a DJ in every group session, a dance party at the end, and yes, there was a hot tub.

In the midst of the luxury and loud music, students were ultimately there to hear from the main session speakers and their personalized session leaders about God.

700 18-22-year-old fraternity and sorority students in a 4-star hotel, some who traveled across the country, to talk about Jesus. The New York Times agreed with me that this was indeed nuts. They even wrote an article on it. Look it up, I swear.

The breakout session I chose was meant for people who were not yet following Jesus. It was the first time I got to ask genuine questions and hear them respond to something other than "just have faith".

I remember being in a room with about 25-30 other students who also weren't sure what they believed in. The room was a little too small for that many people.

Round tables everywhere with nice clothes laid on top of them as if we were at a board meeting. A few things were pinned to the walls but ultimately, this space was not set up with aesthetics or comfort in mind.

Throughout this time, the session leader facilitated the discussion around frequently asked questions, such as 'Why does God allow bad things to happen?'. Mid-weekend, there was a panel of 5-6 older people that we could ask our questions to.

Students were firing off questions and the pace was exactly what you'd expect of a semi-engaged group of college students. I deemed whatever question was asked silly and cut off the conversation.

So, boldly, and frankly rude I had asked, "So essentially what I'm hearing you say is that you want me to let Jesus, a stranger, into my dorm and then once I let Him in, you want me to let Him run my life? Why would I? Why would anyone do that?".

The room fell silent.

Right after, the students kicked into a full-on group-think. Picture full on mob status, loudly stating their affirmation for my question and even patting me on the back.

The panel looked at each other wondering who was going to answer my very abrasively phrased question.

An older man with small, wire-framed glasses and an approachable demeanor spoke up, "You're right, that does sound crazy. Where you're wrong though is that Jesus is not a stranger at all. You can get to know Him by reading Matthew, Mark, Luke, and John. The gospels in the Bible are all about Him and His life, so before you make your decision to let Him in or not, I encourage you to get to know Him there."

It was the first time an adult acknowledged my questions about Jesus. It was the first time someone admitted that the whole idea seemed bogus. It was also the first time though I got an answer that challenged me.

If I could read about Jesus through the lens of 4 of His closest friends, I no longer had an excuse to call Him a stranger. I just had to get to know Him.

That was the first time I thoughtfully engaged with scripture. That weekend was also the first time I heard the gospel. Throughout the weekend in those sessions, I started to think through who Jesus was, if He was real or not and if He was, what that would mean for my life.

The final night at the main session, Beau and Kristina Crosetto spoke about the prodigal son, a story from the Bible in Luke 15.

(If you haven't read it, I would encourage you to, but I will give you the quick and dirty version here.)

A young man asks for his inheritance early, before his father dies. His father, out of the purest and kindness of his heart, agrees and gives his son a ⅓ of everything he has. The son goes out and blows it on nonsense stuff like girls, booze, and parties.

This young Jewish man ends up sad and alone, longing for what pigs eat and decides he has to go home. The son plans to beg his father to allow him to be his servant. Anything is better than the mess he had found himself in.

As he is still a long way down the road, his father runs to meet him in the street. His father immediately gives him a robe and a ring and shoes for his feet. He kills the best calf on the farm and throws a party.

I was, and still am, in awe of this story. Beau and Kristina beautifully explained that this is exactly what God does for us. When we've taken everything He has given us and run off doing whatever we please, He awaits longing for us to come back to Him. When we do choose to come back, He rejoices.

I couldn't believe it. I had run off with everything He had given me, totally ignored all that He has put in my life to do whatever I wanted. Now, these people were telling me I could just come to Him with anything and everything, and He still wanted me? I could not believe it.

Kristina, through tear-filled eyes, invited people to stand from their seats if they wanted to come home to Jesus. To be filled by Him and to stop trying to fill themselves with other things. People all around me stood up and I just couldn't.

Gripping the hand of one of my sorority sisters next to me, my head was whirling with all the failed attempts at filling myself. My heart was burdened by the guilt I felt for all that I had done. I couldn't gather up the nerve to stand.

Kristina asked again though. And again. The third time she asked, something inside me changed, the failed attempts didn't matter as much, the guilt was gone, and I just wanted to run home. I stood with my sister, of course.

In that moment, I felt the presence of the Holy Spirit. My heart shifted and the weight was lifted. I knew, partially because Kristina told me, that God was rejoicing that I had come home. I knew there was a party going on in heaven for me and everyone else that made decisions that night.

My life started changing little by little and I still feel and carry a different fullness about my life to this day. I was a sophomore in college when that had happened.

I have since then led around 15 sorority sisters to Jesus through the Bible study. I went on to work for Greek InterVarsity Christian Fellowship for 5 years after college.

In those years, through God's grace alone, I had the opportunity to plant chapters at Ohio State University, Western Michigan University, and Grand Valley State University where I got to assist in leading 276 students to accept Jesus.

I then went on to be an executive assistant where I got to lead a coworker to Christ, and now find myself working for a small company that I love and am keeping my eyes and ears open for opportunities to weave Christ into the activities there.

In the years since college, I'd conservatively guess that I got to help lead another 100 people to Jesus in restaurants, bars, grocery stores, bathrooms, and anywhere else they would listen.

You see, once I understood that I had the best news ever, I couldn't fathom not letting other people in on the goodness. That's what I want for you by the time you finish this book.

The news that Jesus lived, died, and rose again for us, is the best news ever. I want you to understand that the only response to the best news ever, is being compelled to share with anyone who will listen.

CHAPTER TWO

Who Jesus is to me

I also want us to be on the same page as we start this journey together on who exactly we are talking about. Jesus is the King of King and Lord of Lords. He is the one true Son of God, fully God and fully man.

He is Holy Spirit that gives life to us each day as we rise and each night as we sleep. He is perfect goodness. He is capable of only love because He is Love. He is God Himself made manifest in flesh and bone.

He was made manifest in flesh and bone so that we, people also of flesh and bone, could see God's love and care for us to a much fuller extent. God's ultimate sacrifice came to us through Jesus, His Son.

God empowered Him through Holy Spirit to live a perfect life here on earth, setting an example for what it looks like to be surrounded by temptation and yet never fall to it. Jesus showed us what it looks like to love our neighbor, to be the least of these, and to follow God as the foremost love of our life.

Jesus didn't just live perfectly for us though, He died perfectly for us. He was crucified in a sadistic fashion, humiliated by those in power as well as those who claimed to love Him.

When He died, the veil was torn. A curtain that was too thick for one man to move was torn straight through, giving every person access to the Holy of Holies. When He died, we all gained access to God Himself. He was then buried for three whole days.

He rose from the grave! He rose from the grave. To my joy, when He rose from the dead, He first tells a woman and that woman goes and tells others. He sticks around long enough for many to see that He is indeed alive. He allows the disciples to touch His wounds, He speaks to many.

He also does not leave us alone, just as He promised. He leaves Holy Spirit here, a part of Him, that can and does live in us when invited so that we can keep a direct line to God. So that we can live with God in us! What an honor.

Jesus is the Son of God, part of the trinity, Father, Son, and Holy Spirit. I will use these names for God throughout. I will do my best to be intentional about using the embodiment of God I am actually referring to.

Father is the one who is in Heaven, Son being who is seated next to us and walked in the form of Jesus for 33 years on earth. Holy Spirit who although is like wind is every bit as tangible as Father and Son.

Jesus is wildly important to me because for all the affirmation we seek and those holes we aim to fill, He is the purest satisfaction. He loves us unconditionally, advocates for us without abandon, teaches us mercifully and provides abundantly our hearts deepest desires. Ultimately, Jesus has shown me He is worthy of trust, love, and respect.

Jesus and His life bring me a profound amount of joy. My life has changed for the better due to His influence and the honor of choosing the Holy Spirit.

A few specific examples are as follows...

I am ever more convinced of my worth.

I am ever more convinced of my purpose.

I am ever more convinced of the meaning of life.

I'll expound but I bet you're hooked now- you're welcome.

Worth: Throughout my life, I have struggled to understand why I matter. I have pursued trying to matter in various ways I've already described.

When I came to know Jesus though, and as I continue to learn and understand the ways in which He teaches us, I know my worth.

My worth comes from the fact that Jesus knew me in my mother's womb and chose me to form from the dust of the earth (quite a tough job, I imagine). My worth comes from the fact that thousands of years before I was born, Jesus knew me and loved me.

So much so that He bore every burden I would ever produce and die a painful and merciless death so that I would stand a chance of meeting God the Father in heaven.

My worth comes from the Father's heart that sent His only Son, to begin with, so that all that could be true. Clearly, I am worth a bunch and so are you.

Purpose: I have found myself searching for purpose in life. I'd guess for longer than I remember, but my first conscious memory of searching was as a senior in High School.

I was inspired during a camp that my highest level of impact might be speaking motivationally to students about living with purpose. Over time though, as I pursued that dream, something was not sitting well.

It became clear that it wouldn't ever actually be enough. When I came to know Jesus though, my purpose became clear. In work, it could vary, and continues to, but in life, my purpose is undoubtedly to bring Jesus fame through loving Him and loving others. I felt relieved even as I wrote that.

My purpose, our purpose, is so simple and beautiful - to bring Jesus fame through loving Him and loving others. Now that I can do.

Meaning of Life: I think to some extent, every human wonders "what is the meaning of life?". Over time, I've become more and more convinced that it is to know God.

I hope that provides as much relief for you as it does for me. Given that purpose, I have something thrilling to wake up for each day. Given that purpose, the pressures of this world lose their draw.

Given that purpose, I have a blessed confidence that I absolutely can not mess this up.

SECTION 2

WHY

CHAPTER THREE

Elevated Surfaces

Over the years, I've come to understand that the Lord wants to speak to us about everything. The Lord speaks to all of us in different ways. Personally, I think our communication pattern is constant.

It's almost like there is a sort of background music in my head running at all times. That background noise is primarily just me asking Him to help me interpret what's going on in the world around me.

The first time I ever heard His voice, He asked me to change the radio station I was listening to. The lyrics were sexual at best, vile at worst, and He wanted me to change it up.

I did and what it flipped to was a song titled "Better Than I Used to Be" and that lyric was precisely what was playing.

He then told me I could listen to whatever, so I switched the station back lovingly laughing at His care for the details.

As I did, I could *not* listen to that song anymore. He had elevated my understanding of what I could be because of who He is. It wasn't just about the song, it was about what influences I would allow into my heart and my life.

I could be better, I could choose to be better. That day I chose to see things from a newly elevated surface.

The Lord has spoken to me extensively about elevated surfaces since then. I'm sure it is partially due to my affinity for playing games on the furniture and dancing on chairs, stages, and tables.

I've always liked being elevated physically and metaphorically. Physically, I have always been partial to it because I could see what was going on around me. I won't try to hide that, I also just love having fun! I love helping other people have a blast too.

It's not just that though. I'm 5'5 and although that's technically "average" it has never been helpful at concerts or grocery stores.

Being on an elevated surface allows me to see what is going on and to have some sense of control. It allows me to see who is having fun and who might need a hand.

I've never hogged any of my elevated surfaces, it's just not in my nature. I've always wanted the best of everything and to share it once I had my hands on it.

I love that the Lord is kind enough to show me that knowing Him, and living for and with Him, is one of the many elevated surfaces I would have access to. I'm always looking for an opportunity to help someone else up.

I'd be willing to bet that the Lord has a special way of speaking to you. Maybe it's through cooking or music. It could be through worship, prayer, or Bible study. It might be through friends or family members.

He speaks to us in the ways that we can hear Him most clearly and in ways we are most likely to understand.

Understanding your motivation for sharing who He is with others is going to be pivotal as you learn to share Him with others.

For me, it's a matter of knowing that I've got the best view in the house from the most elevated surface He has invited me to, while wanting others right up there with me.

For you, it might be that it's the absolute best news you've ever heard and you can't wait to share it. It might also be that your relationship with Him is the most fulfilling one in your life and you want to share His love with everyone.

Whatever your perspective, it's important that you understand what your thought process is or why you feel like God's love is worth sharing.

Take some time now to think about it. After you've mulled it over, let me help you nail down another mindset that may be more appealing if you don't think it's a bundle of fun to dance on tables.

CHAPTER FOUR

Being Comfy

Now, beyond elevated surfaces, those who know me will tell you I appreciate being comfy more than almost anything in life.

Although I love getting dressed up and having nice pictures, I'm typically the first one to go barefoot at a wedding. I have no shame in showing up in socks and sandals.

When at home (and often in public), there is a 99% chance you will find me in sweats and a ponytail, most often with a blanket.

Oddly enough, tonight, I am making chicken pot pie in a crockpot with homemade biscuits (currently in the oven, the butter smells phenomenal) cuddled up in our best circle couch, with our biggest and softest blanket, and dressed in my most comfortable pajamas.

I *love* being comfy because it allows me to slow down and unwind. When I am comfortable, there are fewer distractions. There's no opportunity when I am comfortable to be swayed away from what I know is right.

When I'm comfortable, what's right comes flowing naturally for me. This makes sense. Same with reading scripture, time and time again, it affirms that the Lord gives us rest and provides us with the most comfort.

Being comfortable is an outward expression, as I am aware that life is not about me. It's also way more preferable compared to the opposite - being uncomfortable. Did you just decide you agree? I thought so.

Honestly though, being comfortable reminds me that I am a valued child of God. It allows me to call on what it means that I am protected, valued, and held by Jesus.

This is how I feel, and how you can feel when you approach people about Jesus. You can feel your absolute best, your most "at home" when you are sharing the gospel with someone. It sounds bizarre but I promise it's true.

Sharing the best part of your life always brings joy. Think about it like this, when people get engaged, what happens? They post that rock on Facebook and think of the best lyric or pun as a caption to make sure everyone they know, knows!

What happens when people get married? On their honeymoon, they upload the pictures.

What happens when people have babies? We delete them as a friend because you are not a baby, Jane, you are supposed to be in your profile picture. Just kidding, kind-of.

My point is, we are quick to share the best parts of our lives with anyone who is paying even the mildest attention.

On the flip side, we are quick to clam up or not even consider it an option when there is an opportunity to share about Jesus. We shouldn't clam up.

I want you, by the end of this book, to feel so comfortable sharing with people about Jesus that it feels just as casual as being on an elevated surface, or in a book nook, or posting that rock of an engagement ring on Facebook.

CHAPTER FIVE

Don't Freak Out

Some of you only mildly relate to my arbitrary examples, but, if you follow and know Jesus, this isn't optional. The Great Commission in Matthew 28 reads

"18 And Jesus came and said to them, "All authority in heaven and on earth has been given to me. 19 Go therefore and make disciples of all nations, baptizing them in the name of the Father and of the Son and of the Holy Spirit, 20 teaching them to observe all that I have commanded you. And behold, I am with you always, to the end of the age."

This command was directly to the disciples, and we are disciples. Disciples are people who seek to know and follow Jesus in all that they do.

Therefore, we go to the ends of the Earth to make His name known, to share with all who will listen about the great difference He's made in our lives. This gets easier with time and practice, I promise.

Also, I should mention that while many of the examples I will provide throughout this book will be "contact" evangelism, meaning I walk up to people and make it my goal to speak with them about Jesus, that is NOT the only way to share the gospel.

We can share the gospel through Bible studies. We can share the gospel as we talk to a coworker about how church was the previous day, and we can share the gospel over dinner with our friends.

Something I want to make abundantly clear is that while we absolutely need our actions to reflect our beliefs, we also need to learn how to speak about our beliefs.

That is the call of Matthew 28. Christ invites us to share about Him verbally with any and everyone that will listen.

Let's talk about it in the context of relationships and sales. If you are pursuing someone, would you just "live life like you're single" in front of them? What would that even look like? Maybe you flaunt your naked lefthand? The idea is awkward to think about.

It would be a lot easier to make more direct moves. If you are attempting to sell something, would you simply demonstrate that item's benefit in your everyday life?

Possibly, but in order to help someone make a purchase, you will have to make the ask.

So many Christians lean on statements like "my life shows Christ, but I don't need to be pushy." Sure, your life might show that you are following Christ, you may truly live a life that begs questions, I hope you do!

But once you get that question, do you know how to respond in a way that will result in leading someone to Christ? If they don't ask questions but you know in your heart that they have been curious and are ready to hear, do you know how to share? Are you willing to share?

I don't know your answers to those questions, but I do know that I hope the answer is yes. Regardless, this scripture is a call from Christ to go and share His life with others and I intend to help you feel more comfortable doing just that.

CHAPTER SIX

Knowing Jesus is to do this

I want to tell you a little about how I've learned more about who God actively is in sharing the gospel than I have in hundreds of Bible studies.

As I mentioned, I worked for InterVarsity Christian Fellowship for about 5 years. I also participated as a student for 3 years!

In my time with IV, I was immensely grateful to learn the art of inductive Bible study. The process of looking at scripture first to figure out what is going on, next to figure out why it matters, and finally, figuring out why it should matter to you.

In 8+ years and hundreds if not thousands of Bible studies, I came to know Jesus in a deeper and more authentic way.

In many ways, those Bible Studies equipped me to share who Jesus is with those around me. What has showed me who He is the most, though, are the interactions I have had with people who don't yet know Him.

As I speak to people in bathrooms, sporting goods stores, restaurants, or on campuses, I see Him come alive around and in me in a way that I don't yet know how I could see if it weren't for sharing who He is with those people.

Each interaction we have sharing who Jesus is with people should be sincere and Spirit-led. Here's an example of what I mean.

It's Fall on a college campus. There's nothing like it. It's basically still summer out. Every person on campus is trying to reinvent themselves *again*. People are more friendly, they are open to almost anyone and anything.

This is a perfect time for some good old fashioned tabling. I would set up a table with my organization each fall and recruit student leaders to come and help find others that might want to start Bible studies.

I'm standing there one day in my striped shirt and trendy sandals feeling like I'm more approachable solely because I look like a student (even though I'm 25 at this point).

A bunch of football players are standing just across the hallway and I am feeling drawn to talk to them. I've been standing there talking with people about Jesus and our organization for a few hours at this point.

I've been rejected enough to feel comfortable with that possibility, so I figure I'd have nothing to lose.

I boldly walk across the hall straight up to this 6'7 ish man (he's a *giant* compared to my 5'5 self) and I confidently ask if he plays football in which he responds, "How did you know?"

"The Adidas gear kinda gave you away (the school was sponsored by the brand), what position do you play?" I responded.

"I actually don't play anymore, I tore my MCL and ACL last season and now I just kind of go for the workout but I won't likely be on the field again."

At this point in our conversation, I am confident that I walked up to exactly the right person. I am feeling led by the Holy Spirit to pray for this man but I know, somehow, that he needs to hear the gospel.

"Have you checked out our material yet? We've been across the hall from you for a bit now, and I noticed you were kind of looking at our displays, want to do that now?"

In the next 3 minutes or so, I shared the gospel with this giant man. I even got him to laugh a few times (epic trust builder), and he was feeling comfortable based on his body language, so I took the leap.

"I think Jesus would love for you to consider following Him, I think though that He would love for you to experience Him. Would you be open to me praying for your knee to be healed? I think Jesus really wants to do that for you."

Side note: *Don't make this stuff up.* If you don't honestly have a hunch or guidance from the Holy Spirit, do not lie. It won't help, I promise.

He says, "Sure! Why not!?"

So we go over to a table and I pray for him, "Holy Spirit, please heal this man's knee back to its original design in

Jesus' Name." I ask if he felt any improvement and he's smiling like a fool. He says, "No, but thank you, I do feel a lot more peace".

Now, I had a bunch of options but the two that were most obvious are to completely stop and wrap up the conversation or to pray and ask the Lord to heal him again. I'll give you one guess what I chose.

"Could I pray for you again? I think peace is a sign that God does want to heal you! Actually, could you test those stairs first and rate your pain on a scale of 1-7?"

He agreed, labored up a few stairs, and said it was at about a 5. I prayed again and naturally, asked him to test the stairs again. He did, and he was at a 2! We celebrated the progress and I offered to pray one more time. He said yes, so I did.

I kid you not, this guy hesitantly took the first step, and then ran up the stairs, ran down them, and ran right past me out and out of the building. I had to chase him to slow him down, invited him to follow Jesus, and asked how I could follow up with Him.

A few things I want to point out to you about that interaction.

First off, I got to know Jesus more clearly in that process. Jesus has a heart to know people, to win their hearts with the depth of His love for them. Jesus did not just want to meet this man, He wanted to meet Him in a way that showed him he cared deeply for him.

Second, He wants to heal people through prayer!

He gives us tangible opportunities as often as we are willing to take them in order for His love to flow through us.

Nothing about that conversation was manipulative or weird, I actually felt bold, alive, and energetic through it.

As we engage with others who don't know Jesus, we need to make sure we are being sincere.

This means that not every interaction we have will be the same. I'm all for having a format to share the gospel and I promise, you will learn that through these experiences shared.

I'm being intentional though, to not teach you a framework for how the interaction can/should go. The truth is, there isn't an answer.

Sometimes you will pray during one of these interactions, sometimes you won't. Sometimes you will talk for an hour, sometimes you will exchange numbers and talk for years. There isn't a formula to this other than to be sincere and make sure we are sharing the gospel.

You can be confident though that there is one thing that is consistent as we share with others about Him. When we let the Lord lead us in interactions, we are guaranteed to see more of Him.

Personally, there is nothing greater I could ask for. I love getting a chance to participate in God's love and am convinced if you can see evangelism that way, you will too.

No matter what you are feeling now about sharing the gospel with others, I want you to acknowledge it.

To do that, I have made space for you through a prayer activity on the next few pages. For yourself, and for your relationship with God, don't skip it.

CHAPTER SEVEN

A Relevant Pause

To know Jesus, and to feel comfortable doing this, is going to require you to practice listening to Him. He speaks to us all in different ways, some through dreams and visions, some in a literal voice, some with scents, some through art written or otherwise, and some through music. He promises though, that He will speak.

John 10:27 says "My sheep listen to my voice; I know them and they follow me."

That's what I want this exercise to lead you into, an encounter with Jesus that allows Him to speak to you about how He wants you to move forward with what the rest of this book is going to ask of you.

Let's set some ground rules for prayer.

1. If it doesn't align with scripture, it's not from God.
2. If it doesn't bring peace or conviction, it's not from God
3. If it doesn't present itself in Godly community, it's at least questionable.

So, here is the question I want you to prayerfully ask Jesus: How can I share who you are to me with the people around me?

The space above indicated silence, so if you need to, set a timer and give Him at least 2 minutes to speak. I trust that He is good and has been waiting for you to lend Him your ear.

Now, if the Lord spoke to you about something completely different than what you asked, *awesome*!

If He didn't seem to say anything, I promise you didn't do it wrong and you're not broken or weird, maybe you just needed some time to slow down and it will take practice.

Imagine not having caller ID, or for some of you, remember not having caller ID. When you pick up the phone without it, you might not know who is calling and or if they are someone you talk to regularly or not.

I want to lovingly challenge you to get to the point with God, that when you pick up the phone, you know who's calling. Keep praying like this as we continue to go through this book. I'll give you space intentionally, but feel free to take it wherever you want or need.

CHAPTER EIGHT

Fruits

Fruits of the Spirit are gifted to us from the beginning and are useful when sharing the gospel with those around us. Galatians 5:22 is where the fruits of the spirit are found. These fruits are listed as joy, peace, patience, kindness, gentleness, and self-control.

As I look at these, I long to have more of each one of them in my life. Now, I'm not stupid enough to pray for them.

Mostly because I know that praying for patience means waiting in long lines. and praying for kindness means being in situations where I just don't want to be kind. I'm kind of kidding.

I truly do long to have more of each of these though. Nothing in my life has allowed me to see more of these come to life in myself than when I'm sharing the gospel with those around me. Story time!

Joy

I don't know if I've ever seen more joy in a student than in Chloe. She was a sophomore at Grand Valley State University who was looking for something for a long time.

I saw, and still see a lot of myself in her. Searching and yearning in everything around her for what could be more.

Jeeze, an amazing woman with charisma, leadership, and talent on the dance floor. She is the girl that everybody wanted to be.

What most people don't know though is that the girl that everybody wants to be is often not that happy with herself. She found herself in a sorority looking for affirmation in all the wrong ways.

Dragged by one of her sorority sisters, Chloe was sitting in front of me one winter, clearly not interested in speaking to me- it was painful.

No matter what I said to engage her in conversation, even when it was not about Jesus, she just wasn't interested.

This is what made it crazy to see over the next few months because she started to engage more and more in her Bible study. Then, eventually, she showed up to a greek conference (the same conference I had come to Faith to 5 years prior).

I've never seen more joy in a student than when Chloe ran up to me after the altar call proclaiming that she was following Jesus for the first time and that she would be attending a month-long Leadership Institute that cost thousands of dollars to learn more about what it looks like to follow him.

I stepped into that joy right alongside her and to this day, I still have trouble recalling a time I felt more joy than in that moment.

Peace

Peace is something I certainly didn't have when I had to pray for this woman. I say "had to" because sometimes that's what it feels like.

I'm walking away from someone in public and I sense the Holy Spirit inviting me to pray for them. I immediately start a fight with Jesus.

Have you ever encountered this? You just know that you're supposed to go talk to someone but you have a million reasons why it's going to be uncomfortable? I do it all the time.

I was walking by this woman in the mall standing near a display rack in a sporting goods store. It was clear that she worked there and that she wasn't having a great day. She wasn't saying or doing anything rudely, she just didn't look very happy.

I, on the other hand, was eating pretzels congratulating myself for not buying anything else in the mall (yes I know that's contradictory), and as I walked by her eating my pretzels I had this strong sense that I was supposed to offer her a pretzel.

I could not believe it. I was supposed to walk back to this woman who is at work and offer her my pretzel which I had already eaten off of. I kept walking,

I made it to the door, and I just could not leave. So... reluctantly, I walked back, and I offered her the pretzel. Shockingly, she didn't want it.

Now, I had two choices: One was to apologize and walk away, the other was to stick it out.

Honestly, I think there's a time and a place for both. I, however, had peace. I knew that something was going on in this woman's life just from the tone of her voice.

So, I said to her, "I feel like the Lord wanted me to come up to you and offer you this to let you know that He sees you."

She looked up at me and said, "Thank you."

I still had peace though so I kept talking. "Really though, the Lord sees you and knows you and cares about you. I don't know what's going on in your life right now but I do feel like the Lord needs you to know that you're loved and that He sees you."

At this point, she almost started weeping. "My grandmother died the other day and the funeral expenses have been a heavy burden on my family. And yesterday my uncle went into the hospital, we don't know how he's doing and I'm still here at work. I needed that word."

I asked if I could pray for her right then and there, she said yes. I explained to her that I would be praying to Jesus, part of the trinity.

She smiled and said "good". I don't know, and I don't know if I'll ever get to know, what impact that had on her that day.

I do trust that the Lord did a work in her life and I'm fairly certain He brought her peace.

Patience

Unsurprisingly, this story isn't so great.

I decided in college that I needed to have a board set up in the student center that would allow me to talk to people that might not normally talk about Jesus.

So, my board was this giant black tri-fold that had a neon yellow middle finger on it and below it in backwards and forwards letters spelt "religion".

I'll pause for a minute so that you can take in how offended you are by me right now.

***

Now that your offenses are aside, I had a lot of success with this. One woman spoke with me and I was able to tell her that the hypocrisy she sees in the church was something that Jesus didn't care for either.

He literally flipped tables over it. She ended up giving her life to Jesus that day not because he flipped tables but because she got to meet the real Him as we looked at scripture together after she stopped at my very controversial board.

This is really where patience shines though. It was during my 4th hour standing in front of this board, and a man comes up to me. He wanted to have a conversation with me about all of the things wrong with the church.

As I tried to engage him to talk about the ways that Jesus agreed with him he just was not having it. As much as I tried to engage with him, show him empathy, and agree with him, he would not hear me out.

There were multiple points where I said I don't think this conversation is getting anywhere and it would be best if we didn't continue. He just wouldn't give up though. At one point I physically walked away from him and he followed me down the hallway.

I don't tell you that story to scare you but to tell you that after 4 hours at this board I had one negative interaction. That day I learned more about patience and developed more patience than I ever could have dreamed.

You might be wondering how I developed patience in that interaction. That man was deeply hurting. If I hadn't stopped and listened to him and try to engage with him for well over an hour, I would not have developed any patience at all.

I'm not saying it was the perfect interaction. I think now I know better when to cut things off when they're just not going anywhere. But I am thankful that the Lord used that interaction to teach me that patience is not just about waiting in store lines. It's about people and we need to be patient with people because He loves us all.

Kindness

As defined by Webster's Dictionary, kindness is the act of being generous, considerate, and friendly. I think there's nothing more generous, considerate, or friendly that you could do other than to share the gospel with someone. Clearly, that's a little swayed by the way I think of evangelism. I believe it's true though.

Talking to people about Jesus has allowed me to see people in a new way. It's allowed me to see people through a lens of kindness that I truly believe only comes from a revelation you receive from Jesus Himself.

I can't see someone without thinking about how much God loves them. This fails to strike me in a meaningful way only when family members are getting under my skin. God is always quick to remind me in those situations.

I think the place where kindness has been shown to me the most in times of evangelism has been when people are really quick to say "thank you"! It seems crazy but it's not uncommon.

Over the course of my years doing College Ministry, I can't tell you the number of students that came to faith.

Well actually, yes I can (276 that I know of), but of those, the ones that came back to me and said "thank you" was amazing. Even if it was just training the person that actually shared the gospel with them, they were still overwhelmed with thankfulness.

In that, I've grown confident that the Lord wants us to share the gospel and that people can, will, and often do see it as a kindness paid to them. It's developed a kindness in me that propels me forward, wanting to share the gospel more and more often.

Gentleness

In the top 100 words my friends might describe me as... "gentleness" would not qualify. Boldness? Yes. Tenacity? Sure. Certainty? Oh, absolutely! Passion? Yep!

Gentleness though... not so much. Evangelism has been a way for me to grow in gentleness that I never could have anticipated. Talking to someone about faith, a very personal matter, requires a sense of gentleness that did not come easily for me.

I remember being asked by a veteran staff that I deeply respect, "Ellaine, how do you see so much evangelism happen on your campus and in your chapter?"

My reply was, "I have no clue how other people don't see this much fruit. Aren't they doing their jobs?"

Clearly, gentleness was not and honestly, is still not my thing.

I'm growing in it though and I'm growing in it largely through what the Lord has made me for, to share His love with others.

The Lord has shown me over time what it looks like to ask people to follow Him gently, but I did not start with that understanding.

The very day I got back from Greek Conference, I barged into my neighbor's dorm and excitedly told him that I had met Jesus and my whole life was different. He was stunned, and although his initial reaction was to laugh, once he realized I was serious, he quickly aimed to shut down the conversation.

He said he was happy for me. I took that, wrongfully, as a cue to tell him 30 minutes' worth of what had happened for me that weekend. Now, my lead strength is empathy, so it was not lost on me that I was making him increasingly uncomfortable.

It also wasn't lost on me that he was actively looking for a way out of the conversation. I determined though that if he knew the truth, that if he could understand what I now understood that his whole life would change the same way mine did.

My neighbor did not commit his life to Jesus that day. This is both a situation where I give myself grace for not knowing what I didn't know and where I wish I could change it. I would love to go back and slow down, ask him more questions, and let it go when he was done having the conversation. I would love to have seen how that year would have gone had I not pushed so hard day one.

As I've allowed myself to be led through situations like that, the Lord develops me more and more in gentleness. I've changed the way I approach people when I am excited, measuring my excitement for what they seem to be receptive towards. I pray that that continues to benefit the people in my life. I have a hunch my mom would tell you she likes me a lot more than she did 5 years ago.

Self-Control

Honestly, this is a tough one. Self-control is something I've never really been strong with. I have a tendency to go all-in or not in it all with specific things. I have tendencies towards getting what I want in ways that are not always the best method. The Lord is still faithful though and has developed me in this area through the gift of evangelism.

For me, this has come through the most with knowing when to quit or not. Part of this requires attentiveness to the Holy Spirit, but the other part requires an understanding that you don't have to know everything. I don't know about you, but I don't think I began to consider that a viable option until I was 25 or so. I'll give you an example of a time when I knew I just needed to let it go.

I was in a bathroom at a bar. No there's no joke here, that's just really where I was. I was washing my hands and this woman started chatting with me about how she didn't see the point in anything, anything at all.

I told her that I understood the sentiment and sometimes felt that way myself but I hold out hope through my faith in Jesus.

She asked how that helped, so I started to tell her. As I did, though, her eyes glazed over like an 8th grader in a physics lecture.

I didn't have any strong inclination to regain her attention, so despite my desire for everyone, ever to pay attention to me- I let it go.

I offered to get her some water and when she refused, I simply walked out.

Walking away from that wasn't easy. She had made a big statement in saying she didn't see the point in anything. I was concerned for her and wanted to help her practically and spiritually. She wasn't primed and ready to hear from me though so I had to let it go.

Sometimes, the Holy Spirit will invite us to press in, and sometimes the Holy Spirit will invite us to walk away. We need to be attentive to what that particular interaction calls for and that requires self-control.

As you choose to engage with sharing the gospel, you will inevitably see more of God's presence develop in you. You will become more like Him every step of the way.

As a people whose lives are centered around becoming more like Jesus, knowing more about who He is, and showing others, I really can't imagine anything better.

SECTION 3

OVERCOMING OBSTACLES

CHAPTER NINE

Tantrums

Throw your tantrum, go ahead, and get it out. I don't say that to be rude or condescending.. I honestly mean it when I say, "Go ahead and get it out of the way".

I know some of you are feeling a lot of feelings right now because I've just told you all these stories and you might not see how you fit into it. If that's you, it's okay.

You don't have to do this like me, that is not the point of me telling you these stories. Let's address some of what might be going on for you.

If you're feeling afraid, that's ok. You are loved, and seen, and deeply known. I've got to ask though, why are you so afraid?

It will be worth it. God's word never falls void. So whether you are speaking directly out of the Bible, directly from the

Holy Spirit, or just directly from the sense you have in your heart - I promise you, it will be worth it.

Honestly, your worst-case scenario here is that they say no. In that case, you can get yourself some pretzels from the mall and you'll be fine.

Never for Numbers

One piece of advice I would be remiss not to give is, don't do it for numbers.

I feel so strongly about this that I recommend you throw a fit if anyone asks you to do evangelism simply for that reason or have taught you in that way. It's a solid reason to not do evangelism at all. Do it quickly though, because you have a life to live and people to help save by introducing them to the truth!

To be clear, I feel strongly about that because the Lord makes it clear that it is He who changes hearts. Not us.

It's not wrong to keep track of who is coming to faith, I've done it and you've seen my numbers in this book already. What I mean is that it is wrong to give credit to ourselves for others coming to know Jesus.

Aside from that, in our day-to-day lives do we really need to keep track of who says 'yes'?

Maybe you keep track with an encouraging sticky note you put in your house, or you potentially put it on Facebook as an encouraging word to show other believers that they can make a difference in people's lives too. I don't know that we need to assign any of our value to it. In fact, I would encourage us not to.

To go out and share the gospel, I am convinced that you don't need a conference to pump you up, but I will help you with an excuse. What I mean by this is, I've seen a lot of friends and coworkers alike get ramped up at a Christian Conference or even a concert and want to tell people about Jesus only after that.

If it takes you those experiences to get hype about sharing the gospel, do it! I'm not sure you've been doing the gospel in a way that's worth doing. Again I don't say that to be demeaning, I just want to make it clear that this can be fun all the time, not just sometimes after attending a "special function".

I'll Even Give You an Excuse

Like I said, I will help you by giving you an excuse. Blame it on me. You heard me!

You have my full permission to say, "I'm reading this book right now and the woman who wrote it challenged me to go out and share the gospel with someone. Could I talk to you about Jesus? She asked me to email her once I do, and she said she actually reads her email, so I feel like I have to."

Don't feel weird pulling this out when or if you get nervous. I've used plenty of excuses from "I have to talk to x amount of people today" to, "hey I have to do this assignment could you be my test subject to make sure that I'm telling the story about Jesus well?".

No joke, both of those have led people to giving their lives to Jesus. Never doubt an excuse's ability to get you in the door or how much more willing people are when they know they could be somehow helping you out.

You can't mess it up. I've already said this, but it's worth giving a paragraph to. There is nothing you can do here that's going to negatively change someone's eternity.

Everything good that comes out of your mouth will be straight from God and everything else... we really don't need to worry about. God is faithful and good and just. He's not going to let you mess this up.

If you're still struggling with the idea, just remember you are not that powerful. Again, I don't say this to demean the work of evangelism. I wouldn't have written a book about how to do it if I believed that it wasn't worth doing.

I've just come to terms with how much more God's capability is, than our own. And how lucky we are to be used as a tool in this way to work alongside Him.

Ultimately, we do this to truly know God Himself. Think about it, when we truly know someone we could talk about them all the time. Whether this is your mother, your father, your guardian, your boyfriend, girlfriend, husband, wife, or child, the people we know the best, we talk about consistently.

I hope through the illustrations given in the gifts of the Spirit stories, you will come to know God better and as a result, be speaking about Him consistently to others.

CHAPTER TEN

Who needs this?

Everyone

Some of you might be asking, "Who do I share this with?". The answer is, there is not a wrong person TO share this with.

There are no barriers to the gospel, and I truly mean that... no barriers.

Don't let someone's outward appearance deter you from sharing. Whether they are wearing other religious garb, or have a mean look on their face, or are talking to someone else, or they're on their phones... there is no reason to not talk about Jesus with them.

Don't let your prejudices get in the way. A woman I deeply respect taught me to not ever say 'no' for someone.

We can't assume that because of the way that someone looks, acts, or speaks that they don't want to hear about Jesus. We also can not assume that we are the wrong person to tell them. So, maybe the best way to sum it up is to just not make any assumptions at all.

"No" is just the beginning, Respectfully

Please do not let one "no" shut you down, this part can be hard. When you're talking to someone and you get to the point where you are asking if they want to follow Jesus and they say no, you're going to be tempted to walk away.

Don't! Don't walk away, A.) that's just super weird because your conversation hasn't actually ended and you've done nothing to end it and B.) there is still an opportunity. You just got the perfect tee up to ask "why?". I try this, at least 3 times.

Some of you just emotionally shut down yet again. I encourage you to take a deep breath. The reason I ask "why" 3 times is because there is typically that much baggage associated with why they said no. Let me give you an example.

I was walking around the Student Union at Grand Valley State University one day. I was brand new to working on the campus and feeling overwhelmed by students who seemed to know where and who they were much better than I did.

I had a goal of giving 10 invitation cards away to our first event on campus. This also meant getting 10 students' contact information before I could go home for the day.

This was a completely necessary boundary for me because I *knew* how uncomfortable I felt about doing the work. I also knew that we would never grow as a witness on campus unless I at least tried.

I also had a friend sitting at a table close by holding me accountable. See? I don't just tell you to do these things, I've done them all myself.

I was looking specifically for fraternity and sorority students since that is who I would be ministering to.

I saw a woman I was almost sure was in a sorority making a poster for the pom squad on campus. I walked up to her and asked her if she was in a sorority, shocked, she said "yes" and asked how I knew.

If you ask anyone I've worked with over the last 5 years, they'll tell you I have a weird sense for these things. Then again maybe it's not that weird, maybe it's another Holy Spirit clue into who I should be talking to.

I failed to get Kristin's contact information that day, but I did give her my number. I knew that I had failed. The likelihood of the young woman reaching out to me after I had spoken to her at random about Jesus was highly unlikely.

I *knew* that when talking to someone about starting a Bible study or about Jesus would be a time I would need to follow up with them down the line, not the other way around.

So after this great conversation, I was worried that I would never see Kristin again. The conversation must have gone a lot better than I had thought because she did text me a few days later.

Kristin grew up in the church but, like so many others, did not understand the gospel. She also did not understand what it meant to believe in Jesus fully and she wanted to learn why.

If you ask anyone I've worked with over the last five years, they'll tell you I have a weird sense of these things. Then again maybe it's not that weird, maybe it's another Holy Spirit clue into who I should be talking to.

I failed to get Kristin's contact information that day, but I did give her my number. I knew that I had failed. The likelihood of the young woman reaching out to me after I had spoken to her at random about Jesus was highly unlikely.

I knew that when talking to someone about starting a Bible study or about Jesus is a time where I would need to follow up with them, not the other way around.

So after this great conversation, I was worried that I would never see Kristin again. The conversation must have gone a lot better than I thought because she did text me a few days later.

Kristin grew up in the church but, like so many others, did not understand the gospel. She also did not understand what it means to believe in Jesus fully and she wanted to learn why.

So, I met with her. I had no agenda other than to study the Bible with her to hopefully show her who Jesus was and why he was worth believing in.

We sat down and it became clear that she needed to know that there was nothing that excluded her from the gospel, that Jesus was real, and still speaks today. So, we studied John 4. John 4 is a beautiful story of the woman at the well.

A woman is out at the well in the middle of the day, the hottest part of the day. The time the least amount of other people would have been there to get water. We know now that this woman was likely doing that purposely to try and avoid the scrutiny of those around her because of her actions during the night.

This woman was "married" to several different men. When Jesus runs into her though, He breaks cultural norms and speaks to her even though she is a woman alone. He speaks to her about living water and what God has to offer her.

He tactfully and with grace calls her out.

He then prophetically speaks what He knows that she has done, been with multiple men and with yet another at the moment.

This tips her off that this man she is speaking to is close to God and she immediately has questions.

You really should read this yourself, but spoiler alert, she is the first person on Earth to learn that Jesus is the messiah (*huge deal*), and you can read about her in church history if you look up "Photini" which we now know her name to be.

Kristin connected with this story not because she had similar habits to this woman, but because of the way Jesus engaged her, again and again. No matter how many questions she had.

We ended up studying this scripture for three weeks in a row for about 90 minutes each time. Each week I would share the gospel with Kristin and each week she would shy away saying, "I don't think I'm there yet" and God continued leading us back to this passage.

Finally, Kristin identified that she couldn't understand why this woman was so slow to receive the water that would allow her to never thirst Jesus offered her. That was my cue.

I explained to Kristin that she and Jesus had started a dating relationship in the last few weeks, they were having fun getting to know one another.

I also explained that she just identified that he was essentially on one knee, offering her and this woman a ring. It was the most beautiful ring she would ever be offered, and she could not understand why this other woman wasn't taking it. I asked why she would not take it either?

She explained to me that she didn't understand what would happen after she took the ring. This was great news for me!

I excitedly explained that she would enter into an engagement, that she would commit to getting to know Him more on her own, in community and that ultimately, she would figuratively marry Him. She would commit to telling people that she was in a relationship with Him and the great things that He's done in her life.

Her literal response was, "That's all?".

Kristin prayed that day to accept Jesus into heart. Over the course of the next three months she started leading a Bible study in her sorority. Each week we would sit down and prepare the specific scripture for that week's Bible Study.

At the end of the semester, we sat down one last time to talk about what had happened throughout the entirety of the Bible study with her sisters. We discovered that she had led 16 of her sorority sisters to Christ.

I asked Kristin how she had done that and she explained that she had shared the gospel every single week as part of the Bible Study.

I asked Kristin what inspired her to do that and she explained that that is just what she thought she was supposed to do. It then occurred to me that each of the three weeks I met with Kristin to read John 4, I shared the gospel.

Right now, even writing that I'm tearing up because God is so good and He will always give us multiple opportunities to accept a ring from him.

When we do, our lives change forever. Once we have that ring and we know how to offer it, it only makes sense to share and offer it as much as possible.

We are invited into sharing Jesus to change people's lives forever. God is so good.

SECTION 4

WHAT

CHAPTER ELEVEN

Table to Stand on or Book Nook to cuddle into

The Great Commission- Matthew 28: 18-20

18 Then Jesus came to them and said, "All authority in heaven and on earth has been given to me. 19 Therefore go and make disciples of all nations, baptizing them in the name of the Father and of the Son and of the Holy Spirit, 20 and teaching them to obey everything I have commanded you. And surely I am with you always, to the very end of the age."

Why take the time and space to include that scripture? Because it makes it abundantly clear that this is a command. This is a non negotiable. Give that information, I want to make sure you get as comfortable as possible sharing this. That's what I intend to help you do and feel over the next few pages.

Regardless of which setting you find more comfortable to successfully share the gospel in, you need to understand it in a very thorough way and how to share it on a very deep level.

The best way to do that is to know the story of God inside and out. That does not mean you have to be a seasoned Christian to understand that you can share, it just means you need a framework to work with. I happen to have one for you.

Life. Death. Resurrection. Holy Spirit. Ask.

That's the framework. If you can remember that you can succeed at sharing the gospel every single time. Let it be known that even mentioning Jesus's name to a nonbeliever carries power and I truly do believe that.

However, if we can address that Jesus lived, died, rose again, and that He gave us the Holy Spirit so that we wouldn't be alone- the person we are sharing with has a far much better chance of meeting Jesus personally.

So, we'll start with some quick explanations with scripture, and then I'll launch you into how I share it.

Life

The reality is that Jesus lived, breathed, and walked with us on this earth. Jesus, as a young man sometimes got under his parents' skin, just like we do! If you're curious about what I am referring to or haven't heard the story, you can read about it in Luke 2:41-51.

Essentially, His family is traveling for Passover in a very large group and His parents assume He is walking with friends and other family. Come to find out, he had spent 3 days in Jerusalem learning from the teachers in the synagogue!

Jesus also spent a normal amount of time eating, sleeping, and taking time alone. For these "human" accounts of Jesus, you can stick your nose into the gospel of Luke and you'll find a doctor's account, and therefore a very human and thorough account of who Jesus was.

I think it's important to know Jesus' background in this regard because it makes my next point all the more important. Jesus was tempted by all the things we are tempted with. He likely got irritable from being hungry, tired, and dealt with parents who inevitably just did not understand.

In the middle of that complicated existence though, He never sinned. 2 Corinthians 5:21, "He who knew no sin was counted as sin so that we might be saved."

We see this more and more clearly as He engages with people throughout His life. The Pharisees are constantly accusing and challenging Him and they can never find Him guilty of anything. It is simply because He wasn't.

He truly and honestly was guilty of nothing. This life allowed Him to completely overcome what came next.

Death

Jesus died a brutal death. A crucifixion designed for pain and humiliation. He was crucified brutally for our sins.

That was the just punishment for the sin of the world. Crazy to think about, the absolute weight of everything ever done wrong was bore on one perfect person.

As people criticized Him on the cross, His response was to cry out to His Father in heaven "Forgive them, Father, for they know not what they do." Luke 23:34. This moment is wildly powerful but sincerely for more reasons than I could explain or even fully understand myself.

What I do know is this though... Jesus made it very clear at this moment that He is indeed our advocate. He believes in us and fights for us, even while bearing the full weight of our sins.

Another notable note on the crucifixion? The veil was torn. Matthew 27:51 would be very easy to overlook if we weren't paying attention.

"And behold, the curtain of the temple was torn in two, from top to bottom. And the earth shook, and rocks were split."

If we don't know anything about temple practices, this just seems like an odd side note. Let me fill you in.

The temple was separated back in the day. Remember before when I described God's Holiness and that He couldn't be in a Taco Bell because of the whole white shirt thing?

Well, the Jewish people applied this reasoning to the temple. Only one person a year could go into the innermost area, believed to be Holy. A place that was blocked off by a curtain that was 6 inches thick.

That curtain was the torn veil. When it was torn, it was a clear sign that there was no longer any separation necessary.

Jesus' death allowed any and everyone to enter His presence. He gave us all His stain protector. We now have His blood covering for us. Again, He is our advocate.

Resurrection

Christ's Resurrection is what takes Jesus from a profit or a great story to definitively God Himself. After Jesus's death, He was in the grave for 3 days and He rose again. He rose again.

That's absolutely nuts! He was in the grave and overcame death. Breath entered His lungs again and with that, He defeated death, not just for Himself, but for all that would one day come to believe in Him.

Him letting Peter touch His wounds, eating with the disciples, chatting with the women (who found Him first!), was all confirmation that He was fully God, fully human, and fully defeated death.

Holy Spirit

Christ promises the disciples before He goes to the cross that He wouldn't leave us alone, that it would be better for Him to go than stay. We've learned the importance of the death and resurrection which is absolutely part of it- also though, the Holy Spirit.

When Jesus made that promise He was referring to the reality that His Spirit would come to stay and guide us here on Earth when He went back to Heaven. What a guy. God thought of everything.

Side note: The Holy Spirit often gets overlooked or left out of our thoughts about God, likely because it's tough to understand. If you find yourself in that boat, it's totally fine. I do want to challenge you to explore the book of Acts. I became more familiar and more comfortable with the Holy Spirit as I read through the book and I am confident that you will as well.

The Holy Spirit acts as a guide in our hearts and in our lives. Holy Spirit acts as a pair of glasses for us to see things in our lives clearly and with perspective, and also our stain protector.

I most notice Holy Spirit's presence when I am tempted to pick up a stain intentionally or when I am ignoring something that Jesus cares for deeply.

Jesus' life, death, resurrection, and impartation of the Holy Spirit is selfish to not share because you have the actual best news ever.

Can you imagine getting engaged and not sharing with a single soul because "it's private?" No. That's ridiculous.

We post pictures on every platform known to man and call every friend and family member and host parties to let them know when we have good news!

Graduated? Announce and party! Engaged? Announce and party! Married? Very expensive announcement and party! Baby? Announce and party! Birthday (where you didn't even do anything)? Announce and party! See the theme there?

Yet for most of us, making the amazing decision to follow Jesus does not get an announcement or a party. I think it should. I think it should involve a DJ, a themed dance party, and a chance to tell some of your best friends.

Granted, I am biased because that's how it went down for me but I am serious! It's stated in scripture that every time someone commits to Jesus the angels rejoice in heaven. Why would we not do the same?

You are going to think I'm nuts but I am comfortable with the fact I'm running that risk already.

If you haven't ever celebrated the fact that you decided to follow Jesus, I want you to announce and celebrate right now, whatever that looks like for you!

Want to call your parents and thank them for raising you to believe? Please, go for it! Want to dance on your bed and text 10 friends? Do it! Want to get yourself a sundae with your very best friend or spouse? Please, go!

Following Jesus is always worth celebrating. That is why I took my friend Georgie to get sundaes and we played music so loud in the car my ears rang all night after she committed her life to Jesus!

Celebrating for our own salvation is step 1, step 2 is to step out and share what it is we are so excited about! You've got the foundational understanding, so keep reading to hear how I do it. (It involves Taco Bell and a proposal.)

CHAPTER TWELVE

My Version of the story

Just below you will read exactly how I share it, it's not the best way, it's just an option. It's also not going to be totally accurate because I do pause for questions and encourage you to have your group reflect on these questions throughout.

My version of the story

As Christians know it best, the world was created perfectly. It wasn't just perfect it was Holy. Holy is one of God's primary characteristics (Holy is essentially next level perfect).

So, imagine how unattainable perfect is, now multiply that by approximately infinity, and you get Holy. That is what God is and that's how He initially created the world, and us, to be. We know though that we have done things to mess that up. We know that because the world we live in currently, as we breathe and sit here right now, we definitely know it's not perfect.

An interesting piece of God being Holy is that He cannot be in the presence of anything that is unholy. It's basically like wearing a white shirt into Taco Bell, it's something you just don't do if you are wise.

So, to put it into perspective, the world we live in now is some sort of Taco Bell. We have sauce flying around us everywhere in the form of unpleasantries. These unpleasantries range from murder and unjust war, to lying to our parents, or stealing penny candy. Each of these unpleasantries makes the world a tougher place to live in.

We have to own that to some extent. The fact is that we contribute to the junk. If you think about it such as unpleasantries are like a sauce spill, a murderer spill will dirty your shirt just as much as the spill created from stealing a candy bar.

We don't need to get into a theological debate about this, I want to make it clear that we all spill sauce on a nice white shirt more often than we even know.

*Pause and ask for questions. A great question to ask would be if anyone in your group has gotten any stains lately, and or if they've done anything to cause a spill.

As these unpleasantries mount higher and higher though, God's primary characteristic aside from Holiness is that He's loving. A loving Father can't leave his children such a gross picture. So, he doesn't.

He sends His own Son, Jesus, fully God and fully human, to come into the world to show us what it looks like to be in the middle of all these unpleasantries and how to not fall into any of them.

Jesus lives a perfect life, He's walking around Taco Bell in a perfectly white shirt and never gets a darn thing on himself. He sets an example of what a stain protector can and should look like.

This all means that when Jesus died, when He was crucified on the cross brutally, He was able to die a perfect death. Scripture explains that He bores every sin on the cross.

That means every spill we've ever had, every unpleasantry we have ever committed, was all taken care of, was removed from us on the cross. Those are not things we have to bear anymore. He isn't asking us to walk around looking all nasty covered in mild sauce.

*Pause and ask if there are questions. A good one is to ask if anyone feels like they are walking around with stains on them that they wish they could get rid of.

If the story ends there, Jesus sets a wonderful example and covers our butts, or I guess to stick with the analogy, our shirts.

That's not all He does though, He actually rises from the grave. He comes back proving furthermore that He is God. He who joins God in heaven and sits at His right hand.

There, He advocates for us. He is our mediator. He is so much more than that, but man am I thankful that He is that as well.

As our mediator, He promised to never leave us alone and He sends the Holy Spirit to do that for and with us. Holy

Spirit is like the wind that you can always feel, and is always guiding us.

When we choose, the Holy Spirit can enter our hearts and change the way that we live as we consult him for guidance continually. It allows us to read scripture in a way that's similar to putting glasses on for the first time.

Holy Spirit often acts as our stain protector keeping us away from any spills to begin with. He also helps us to know how to clean them up when it does happen.

I don't know a single person that wouldn't want to have a stain protector magically on them inside of a Taco Bell. Let's be real. Something that would cost you nothing and simultaneously give you everything you need to live in this world without a single stain.

That's what and how Jesus acts as. The best offer you'll ever get is already on the table before you. You can know the one true God and accept the Holy Spirit into your heart by acknowledging that you too believe it's true that Jesus lived, died and rose again. With and through that, the Holy Spirit becomes your stain protector.

CHAPTER THIRTEEN

The Ask

So, what do you think about everything I've shared with you so far?

That's interesting, do you think there is any part of Jesus' life you still have questions about committing to or believing in?

Awesome! I think of Jesus' life, death, and resurrection as a sort of proposal to us. Frankly, it's the best one I think anyone could ever receive.

So I have to ask, where are you at in your relationship with Jesus-

Are you not interested and just watching from afar?

Are you dating and getting to know Him but unwilling to trust and believe in Him?

Are you engaged, fully believing in Him, but not quite ready to commit to the extent everyone knows about it?

Or are you married, believing, committed, and willing to tell everyone?

Wherever you are at, awesome! If you're engaged, that's super awesome! I love that you said you believe in Him but you're not sure what it looks like to fully commit to Him in marriage.

The reality of that is you commit to making Him the primary relationship in your life, learning more about Him in scripture, and a part of community within a church. Would you want to pray now that you would be that committed to Him?

Yes? Awesome!!!

Will you pray with me?

Jesus, we acknowledge that you lived, died, and rose again for us and our stains. Jesus, would You act as our stain protector and best friend for the rest of our lives? We accept Your Holy Spirit into our hearts to guide us in our lives of following you. You are our Lord and Savior, Jesus. We are thrilled to be married to You. Amen.

End Scene

Disclaimers

It won't always go the way that you just read. Sometimes it will be a much more blunt "no" that you will receive. Sometimes, you will still be talking with that person about it years later.

Sometimes, it will take them hearing it from someone on a stage and you'll wonder why they couldn't hear it from you when you said the exact same thing just before.

The reality is though, you need to make the ask and then ask questions around their answer. I'll give you another example.

I was exhausted. I had just come off of a fun holiday weekend with my family and was settled in my much too small seat on a flight to Los Angeles. I had my headphones in and was resting against the window ready to pass out for the next 4 hours.

In comes my seat neighbor. He immediately started talking with me and I was less than thrilled.

I also had a hunch that this guy needed to know Jesus, so I chose to wake up and engage.

I learned that he was an actor on a popular Netflix show and that he played soccer at Michigan State.

Naturally, he asked what I do and I told him I worked with fraternity and sorority students helping them to start Bible studies with their friends and understand who Jesus is in their lives.

That is where he shut down. It was abundantly clear so I took a left turn in our conversation and asked what he was involved with in college and talked with him about a number of other things.

Eventually, I noticed him loosen up again, and asked if he was ever involved in church and whether or not he knew what the word "gospel" meant.

He, like many others I've asked that question with, said, "Yeah, like music."

I told him that yes, it absolutely is sometimes music but it's also the story of Jesus' life and ask if I could share that with Him.

I clarified that I wanted to share it not because I was assuming he didn't know it or hadn't heard it, but because a fresh perspective on an old story sometimes helps us see it in a new light.

I shared about Jesus' life, death, and resurrection in a matter of maybe four minutes.

By the 90 second mark, I could tell he was annoyed. I threw in a Taco Bell joke, he lightened up.

By the 3 minute mark, I could tell this probably wasn't going anywhere. You know what I did in the end? I asked where he was at in his relationship with Jesus.

Why did I still ask even though it was apparent he wasn't very interested? Because it couldn't hurt.

When he responded, it was not a yes. He gave me a lengthy explanation of his disinterest in religion and we got to have a decent conversation about that.

Before I let it go, I asked if he wanted a relationship with Jesus. He wasn't interested. I let him know that if he ever changed his mind, he could pray and invite the Lord into his heart. I knew full-well that the likelihood of him doing that any time soon was slim.

I'm also convinced that him knowing it was an option is a much better place than the alternative.

This conversation was uncomfortable and this guy wasn't super interested. I tried to navigate the gray in it though.

I respected his boundaries and still stuck with the truth that Jesus is worth knowing. I didn't know what was going to happen and even though I had clear signs, I didn't make assumptions.

I've learned through trial and error though, the worst-case scenarios are the ones where I don't ask at all and am left wondering "what if"?

Please, don't leave yourself wondering "what if". Just go ahead and do it scared.

You have to. You have to. Making the ask is pivotal. Just like on a date, in a proposal, during a sale, or to wrap up a fundraising appointment you have to make the ask.

I mentioned at the beginning of this book that some people get squirrely about this part and I get it, it's where you might get rejected.

The reality though is this ask is not about you at all, it is about the other person and the opportunity they have to know about and commit to the best proposal they will ever receive.

It would be cruel not to ask.

CHAPTER FOURTEEN

Curveball

Prayer. Yep. We talked about it before and we are talking about it again because it is that important that we know we need to be praying as we talk to people about Jesus.

Whether we are talking to our parents for years or a person we met in a restaurant for 5 minutes, we need to be praying throughout the process of it.

I spoke to you a little about how the Lord is consistently speaking to me and I to Him sort of like background music in my head.

This is a learned practice and one that I hope you can choose to engage in your own way as you share His story.

Sometimes, this will be pausing to pray in your head between explanations. Sometimes, you will have a direct sense from the Holy Spirit about what to say or where to take the conversation next. Sometimes, it will be for peace or confidence to continue the conversation.

Now would be a good time to go back to chapter 7 and do that exercise again.

Really, go do it.

***

As I've engaged with the Lord over the years I have come to understand that I truly need and desire Him in everything I do.

Particularly telling others about Him, I've leaned heavily on this prayer from St. Patrick.

I want to encourage you to practice 'Lectio Devina' or the practice of 'divine reading' as you read through this prayer. There are many ways to practice this but what I recommend are the steps below.

1. Breathe for 10 seconds, then just read through the prayer. Breathe for 10 seconds again.
2. Breathe for 10 seconds, then read through and ask yourself what stands out to you. Breathe for 10 seconds again.
3. Breathe for 10 seconds, then read through considering what God might be communicating to you specifically through this exercise. Finish by breathing for 10 seconds.

"Christ with me,
Christ before me,
Christ behind me,
Christ in me,
Christ beneath me,
Christ above me,
Christ on my right,
Christ on my left,
Christ when I lay down,
Christ when I sit down,
Christ when I arise,
Christ in the heart of every man who thinks of me,
Christ in the mouth of everyone who speaks of me,
Christ in every eye that sees me,
Christ in every ear that hears me."

My hope as you engaged with that practice is that you got a bit more understanding on what hearing from the Lord looks like and also that you got to hear from Him directly.

I want to encourage you that what you are doing when you pray throughout your times of telling others about Jesus, is truly letting power run the program. What does that mean? When we decide that we want to share who God is, and letting Him lead us, He rejoices.

I wonder though if He watches from right beside us, at first holding the handlebars like a father teaching a wobbly child how to ride a bike without training wheels for the first time. I like to think so.

The way that we can feel safe is to recognize that He is guiding us by chatting with Him throughout our wobbly experience. He's holding on and even if we fall, He will be right there to pick us

CHAPTER FIFTEEN

Let Him stick His flag in us, not ours in others.

This is what we need to allow for throughout the whole process of our lives.

What I mean by this is we don't ever want to help people see a version of Jesus that isn't who He truly is, which means we need to know Him and know Him well.

We also need to have our hearts fully invested in Him. This doesn't mean we need to be all cleaned up before we start sharing Him with others.

In contrast, people are more compelled to listen when you are willing to share that you are indeed a mess who is still figuring it out.

What is true though, is that we need to consistently and constantly be setting our eyes on the truth of who He is and allowing ourselves to be corrected and guided by the Holy Spirit and scripture.

This needs to happen for us to be effective communicators of the gospel and effective followers of Jesus. If you are finding yourself in a tough spot, that is ok. It does not disqualify you from sharing the gospel.

A few years ago, a friend who was far too young passed and I remember sitting at a bar with another friend talking about her and what I would miss. Next to us was this very rowdy group of construction workers, and they were very bold in offering us drinks and conversations.

Naturally, I shared with them that we were working with college students to share who Jesus is and this started an hour-long conversation that although I did not feel emotionally equipped for, the Lord was gracious enough to lead me through.

I shared the gospel on a napkin over whiskey at an upper peninsula bar with a burly construction site leader and you know what? I think his heart shifted towards Jesus that day. Sometimes, we don't have it in us, but when we are weak, God is strong.

Other times though, we are on a mountain top high in our relationship with Christ and can make less-than-stellar decisions about how, when, or where to share the gospel. Let me set the scene for you of a time I did this in college.

I was at my favorite fraternity house. Party of a lifetime. Hundreds of people milling around in theme attire. Some dancing, some standing, some making attempts to hit on their crush of the night. Some, mostly just me, talking to people about Jesus.

Now hear this, what I am not saying is that we should not talk to people about Jesus when there is alcohol involved. Jesus drank wine and people are more willing to talk about the tough stuff when they are drinking.

We need to know and respect a line though, and that is where I failed here.

Chad was wearing a brightly colored hat from a camp that was popular in Michigan and very well-known for its Christian influence. One of those camps with the blob in the lake and a zip line where a ton of kids gave their lives to Jesus for the first time.

Chad is walking away from me and barreling up the stairs, but I notice the hat so I follow him and start asking about it.

He made it clear pretty quickly that he was not down to chat about it when he immediately said, "Yeah, I hated that place."

Oops. I probably should have let it go then and there. He had a fair amount to drink, I was not getting any sense from the Lord to press in. I was determined though. "Why did you hate it? I know a lot of people that passionately loved going there."

For the next 10 minutes or so Chad cursed up a storm and huffed around his too-small room shoving clothes around on his bunk bed telling me about his experiences at this camp.

He had gone with pretty strong faith and whilst there, asked some questions. The answers he got were demeaning and hurtful. His sincere curiosities were met with trivial responses and platitudes such as "just have faith".

While that is not an inherently awful response, it's certainly not an appropriate one for anyone sincerely seeking an answer to a question they deemed worth asking.

Chad began to cry. What did I do? Kept pushing.

To be honest, I don't remember what I asked but I do remember that for the next 40 minutes or so, Chad got more and more upset and I just kept pushing, hoping to find the hole in his reasoning, completely ready to stick my flag in him.

"Chad, I'm sorry. I'm sorry because you needed someone to hear your hurt and pain. You didn't need a pious woman in the middle of a party in your home to poke at a wound until it bled and then dig around in it until it hurt enough for you to cry. I didn't know what I was doing and I'm sorry."

I want you to know that I'm not perfect and I don't pretend to be anymore. Christ's love is perfect though and perfect for you. Your questions are valid and you deserve answers. If you ever decide you want to sit and chat or talk over the phone, I'm still here for you.

Sometimes, we might need to apologize on the spot. I wish I had that day. I trust God though that Chad is a top priority for Him and I am not powerful enough to break that love up.

CHAPTER SIXTEEN

Your Plan

It would be wise now to stop and take the time to think through how this will play out for you. How will you feel the best communicating Jesus' life, death, resurrection, and receiving of the Holy Spirit in which you choose?

Would you prefer to talk about it through the lens of a relationship? Going from flirting, dating, engaged, then married?

Would you prefer to talk about it through the lens of strict scripture? Potentially following the ever-popular Romans Road?

Would you prefer to weave in relatable jokes about Taco Bell or some other popular social reference?

I can tell you this, regardless of what you decide, you can do this and once you do, it will become much easier.

I'm going to ask 4 questions and leave space below for you to answer them. This activity is meant to help you understand how exactly you might share the gospel.

1. How will I communicate our need for Jesus?
2. How will I communicate that need is fulfilled by Jesus' sacrifice?
3. How will I communicate that we have a choice in accepting that and receiving the Holy Spirit?
4. How will I communicate that when we choose to accept all of that, we should communicate it with others?

SECTION 5

GO NOW!

CHAPTER SEVENTEEN

Now

Seriously. Now. Go, and do it! Find a partner, find an excuse, and or use me as one! You know me well enough now to use me as an excuse, that's why we began this book where we did, for me to tell you my story.

You now know that any place is an appropriate place to share the gospel.

The fruits of the Spirit will inevitably multiply within you as you share the gospel with those around you. You will become more like Jesus through the process.

You now know how to hear from God better and how to communicate His story effectively.

You've practiced listening to His voice and have a specific practice to return to when you'd like (Chapter 7).

You've read exactly how I share with others and hopefully gleaned ideas of your own on how to do so.

You've also taken time to think about how this will work for you and come up with a tangible plan.

You know the reasons why nothing should hold you back.

I remember a few years back I got a room of 20 fraternity and sorority students who barely knew each other to practice this twice and then had sent them out at 9:30 pm around the university center and library to share the gospel.

I sat in the room, waited, and prayed. I gave them 10 minutes to do it, so when they left the room they ran.

When they came back, one group actually brought someone with them. This kid was kind enough to let me ask in front of the room what happened, how he felt when they came up to him, and how he responded.

He committed his life to Jesus that night.

10 minutes of training, a 10 minute challenge, and a question. That's all it took for this man's eternity to be changed. Praise God.

You have more than 10 minutes, what are you waiting for?

A Note From The Author

This book didn't take long to write. Hopefully, that did not show.

I don't think it took that long because it flows straight out of my heart in which was designed by God.

As I continued to live my life after the formal writing process was over, I continued experiencing stories that I would think, "I have to share this in the book!".

The reality though is that you don't need to hear another one of my stories. You don't need one more inspirational word to lead someone to Jesus. You need to commit to going out and doing it yourself.

Commit to speaking at that seminar you were invited to.

Commit to finally telling your parents that you love Jesus and why.

Commit to sharing the gospel once a week until you feel comfortable doing so, once a day is the new standard. I did that in college for a semester, ask me about it later.

If you, your church, your small group, or your college ministry are considering using this as a tool to learn, I'd love to hear about it and I'd love to help.

Let me know how it goes by emailing me at **dontbeweirdstories@gmail.com** or text **8102471973**!
I will reply and celebrate both wins and failures with you!

Thanks for reading,
Ellaine Ursuy

Made in the USA
Monee, IL
21 August 2021